THOROUGHBRED HORSES

Dorothy Hinshaw Patent

HOLIDAY HOUSE / NEW YORK

Library of Congress Cataloging in Publication Data

Patent, Dorothy Hinshaw.
Thoroughbred horses.

Bibliography: p.
Includes index.
SUMMARY: Text and photographs present the history
of thoroughbred horses, how they are trained to be some
of the fastest horses in the world, the competitive
sports in which they participate, and some well-known
horses.
1. Thoroughbred horse—Juvenile literature.   2. Race
horses—Juvenile literature.   3. Horse sports—Juvenile
literature. [1. Thoroughbred horse.   2. Race horses.
3. Horse sports]   I. Title.
SF293.T5P38   1985   636.1′32   84-48742
ISBN 0-8234-0558-3

For Barbara Baker and others like her, who love racehorses for their spirit and heart.

Contents

THOROUGHBRED HORSES

*Thoroughbreds are bred for racing. The horses are wearing
blinders, which prevent them from looking sideways.*
KNIGHTS OF AK-SAR-BEN

1

Bred for Speed

Most horse breeds were developed for some kind of work—plowing fields, pulling wagons, rounding up cattle, or carrying warriors. But not the Thoroughbred. This horse was bred for one thing only—speed. Throughout its history, the Thoroughbred horse has been first and foremost a racehorse. The modern Thoroughbred is beautiful, spirited, and fleet-footed. It is the fastest animal alive at running the mile.

Although the Thoroughbred was developed mainly with an eye to racing, the resulting horse has proved talented at other sporting activities, too. Thoroughbreds are used as polo ponies, as jumping horses, and as mounts for the riding event called dressage. The Thoroughbred, because of its special characteristics of speed, endurance, and size, has also been used to develop and improve other horse breeds around the world.

Traits of the Thoroughbred

The majority of Thoroughbreds are large horses. The height of a horse is measured in "hands." A hand is four inches. The height is taken from the ground to the top of the shoulders, called the "withers." While an Arabian is usually under 15 hands and a Quarter Horse is rarely more than 16 hands, the average Thoroughbred is about 16 hands high. Thoroughbreds weigh from 900 to 1,200 pounds. They have muscular, sloping shoulders and powerful hindquarter muscles that propel their ground-covering stride. Their deep chests hold very generous lungs and a large, strong heart. Thoroughbreds are spirited horses with a desire to run. Their "hotblooded" bodies require plenty of food to keep them going; a fat Thoroughbred is rare.

One of the most important traits of the Thoroughbred is difficult to define. "Heart" is a special combination of competitiveness and determination that characterizes all great racehorses. Racing hurts, for it involves pounding around the track as fast as possible, even when strength is running out. In order to win, a good racehorse must get past any pain and any temptation to slow down, and no jockey, no matter how competent, can force a horse to go faster or farther than it wants to. But a horse with heart will go all out to win even if it must suffer in the process.

The Thoroughbred has powerful muscles
to help it run fast.
NORTHERN CALIFORNIA THOROUGHBRED ASSOCIATION

4

Thoroughbred History

Where did the Thoroughbred horse come from? There are many romantic stories associated with this question, but we actually know very little about the early development of the breed. In England during the late seventeenth and early eighteenth centuries, horses, especially stallions, were introduced from the Middle East to improve British breeds. Some of these horses were Arabians, but others belonged to different Eastern breeds such as Barbs. The origin of all of these animals is largely unknown. The peoples of the Middle East had been developing fast, hardy horses with great endurance for many generations. In the region that today includes northeastern Turkey and part of the Soviet Union, for example, several different breeds were used for racing and for war.

It is hard for us today to determine the exact breeds of the stallions sent to England centuries ago. It is even more difficult to find out about the mares used in the development of the Thoroughbred. Although a few may have come from the East, most did not. Good mares were treasured by their owners in the Middle East, so they were rarely sold. The mares used in the early development of the Thoroughbred were more likely native English horses of various types. A racing breed called the Galloway and another called the Norfolk are specifically mentioned in old breeding records. Unfortunately, both these breeds have disappeared, so we have no modern examples to show us how they may have looked. Early drawings of these horses are probably not accurate. Other English horses, such as the popular riding horse called the Cob, were almost surely involved in producing the early racehorses that led to the Thoroughbred as well.

Although our knowledge of Thoroughbred origins is sketchy, three particular Eastern stallions are considered the founders of the Thoroughbred breed. The first to reach England, in 1689, was called the Byerly Turk. We know very little about this horse, except that he was a black war horse captured by a Captain Byerly during a battle in Turkey. The second of these three stallions is called the Darley Arabian. We do not know if this horse was actually of the Arabian breed, but he was bought in Syria in 1703 or 1704 by Thomas Darley and brought to England.

Many legends surround the third of these horses, the Godolphin Arabian, also called the Godolphin Barb. Again, we do not know his exact breed. There are several differences between modern Arabians and Barbs. Since these differences probably also existed in the eighteenth century, we cannot be sure what the Godolphin stallion looked like. A well-known children's book, *King of the Wind*, by Marguerite Henry, is based on the legends surrounding this fine stallion. He was supposedly sent as a gift to the king of France from a North African ruler and was said to be accompanied by a mute groom, but there is no proof that this is so. Whatever his origins, the stallion did end up as an abused cart horse on the streets of Paris. A kindly Quaker named Edward Coke purchased him and nursed him back to health. Eventually, the horse came to the breeding farm of Lord Godolphin in England. There, he was bred several times to a fine mare named Roxanna. The resulting offspring were especially good racehorses, and the Godolphin's reputation was established.

Actually, all three of these stallions got their reputations through the results of breeding, since they themselves never raced. Each of them led, through what is called the "tail-male" line, to one of the three great racehorses that started the Thoroughbred breed. The tail-male line follows only the male ancestors of a horse. It traces the horse's sire (father), then the sire's sire (the horse's grandsire), then the great-grandsire, and so forth. The tail-male line is considered very important in Thoroughbred breeding, for every Thorough-bred today can be traced this way back to Herod, Matchem, or Eclipse, the three founders of the Thoroughbred breed. Many other Eastern stallions besides the Godolphin Arabian, Byerly Turk, and Darley Arabian were important in pro-

This is Eclipse, the most important founding father of the Thoroughbred horse.

ducing the early Thoroughbreds, but these others cannot be traced through the tail-male line. Because of their importance, the Byerly Turk, Darley Arabian, and Godolphin Arabian are called the "foundation sires" of the Thoroughbred breed.

Matchem was the earliest of the three first Thoroughbreds. He was a grandson of the Godolphin and was foaled in 1748. Matchem was tall for a horse of the time, almost four inches taller at the shoulder than either of his parents. Matchem had the look of the Thoroughbred, with high withers and strong shoulders. He was a successful racehorse and a fine stud who produced many good racehorses. Matchem's descendants include such famous horses as Man O' War, perhaps the greatest racehorse that ever lived.

Man O' War was a great favorite of the people. In addition to being an outstanding racehorse, Man O' War produced top offspring, including the 1937 Triple Crown winner, War Admiral.
KEENELAND-COOK

Herod was the second of these stallions to come along. Herod was foaled in 1758 and was a great-grandson of the Byerly Turk. Herod's birth was the result of careful breeding by a famous horseman of the time, the Duke of Cumberland, and it paid off. Like Matchem, Herod was tall and powerfully built. He, too, was a fine racehorse and a good sire. Although the tail-male line of Herod produced fewer horses than that of the other two, his breeding resulted in many fine mares. The blood of Matchem is present throughout the female lines of great Thoroughbreds today.

The most spectacular and productive of the three first Thoroughbred stallions was Eclipse. His name fit him well, for his influence almost overshadows that of any other horse in Thoroughbred history. Eclipse was foaled in 1764. He was a great-great-grandson of the Darley Arabian and, like Herod, was the result of thoughtful breeding by the Duke of Cumberland. Eclipse was a huge horse, almost 17 hands high. Because of his ungainly appearance—his hindquarters were an inch taller than his withers—Eclipse was bought as a yearling for a modest sum. Eclipse proved difficult to train, too, for he was ill-tempered. But once he began racing, his incredible superiority was clear to everyone. He was never defeated and had to be retired from the track after only twenty races because no one would put up a horse against him!

DIOMED

Eclipse proved just as outstanding in fathering racehorses as in performing on the racetrack. Approximately 80 percent of Thoroughbreds today can be traced back to Eclipse through the sire line, and most of the rest carry his blood through the female side.

The fact that Eclipse was the result of careful breeding led breeders to realize the importance of bloodlines in producing superior horses. A few years after Eclipse died, the standardization of the Thoroughbred breed began with the establishment of the *British General Stud Book* in 1791. The *Stud Book* is the record of the breeding of all Thoroughbreds in England, and it was not long before listing in the *Stud Book*

Lexington, a great American racehorse and sire of racehorses, was born in 1850 and died in 1875. Unfortunately, his bloodlines were allowed to die out, and no descendants of this fine horse are alive today.
FROM THE COLLECTION OF THE NATIONAL MUSEUM OF RACING, INC., SARATOGA SPRINGS, NEW YORK

required that a horse be a descendant, through the tail-male line, of Matchem, Herod, or Eclipse. In the United States, Thoroughbreds are registered in the *American Stud Book*, which was first published in 1868. Like English Thoroughbreds, all American ones must be traced back to the same three stallions through the tail-male line.

Many of the American horses on the female side, however, have different origins from those in England. The English Thoroughbreds went back to the three foundation sires in the female as well as the male line. But many of the early American Thoroughbred mares were half-breeds, which could only be traced through the tail-male line to the foundation sires. From 1913 to 1949, the *General Stud Book* just accepted horses that traced back to the foundation sires in all lines. This kept most American racehorses from being considered "Thoroughbreds" by the British. By 1949, American Thoroughbreds were clearly superior in general to English ones, so the British changed their rules again and allowed American horses to be included in the *General Stud Book*. Since then, many American horses have been used to improve the English Thoroughbred. In fact, in October, 1984, Queen Elizabeth II personally visited Lexington, Kentucky, to choose American stallions to match up with the twenty-one broodmares she keeps in Great Britain.

2

Breeding and Raising Thoroughbreds

Raising Thoroughbred horses is "big business" in the United States today, as well as in other countries such as England and France. The American Thoroughbred industry involves an investment in horses and property of over a billion dollars! Thoroughbreds are expensive, and raising them is also costly. The most important item in determining the value of a Thoroughbred horse is its bloodlines—its ancestry. If a horse's dam (mother) and sire (father) were great racehorses, it is very valuable, and so are its own offspring even before they have raced. A fine Thoroughbred broodmare—a mare used for breeding—can be worth $3 million or more. And breeding that mare to a great stallion can cost over $100,000! The resulting young horse may sell for over a million dollars.

When a stallion has proved himself a good racehorse, he is retired to stud. This means that he stops racing and his value is now measured by the racing and breeding success of his offspring.

The owner of a stallion charges the owner of a broodmare a "stud fee" for mating her to the stallion. A mating to a stallion that raced well and has good bloodlines will cost much more than mating a mare to a lesser animal. Horses that have won one or more of the classic American contests for three-year-olds which make up the Triple Crown are particularly in demand.

The first of the three races of the Triple Crown is the Kentucky Derby, run at Churchill Downs racetrack in Kentucky on the first Saturday in May each year. The Kentucky Derby was established in 1875 as a way of showing off the fine Thoroughbreds raised in Kentucky. It was modeled on the famous British classic race called the Epsom Derby. For the first ten years, the Kentucky Derby was a popular race. But in 1886, a powerful racehorse owner from New York, James Ben Ali Haggin, was insulted by Derby officials. He promptly withdrew his horses, and other owners from the North joined him in ignoring the Derby. From then on, both the Derby and Churchill Downs began to decline in influence and popularity.

The fortunes of the Kentucky Derby were revived when a clever promoter named Matt Winn became the manager of Churchill Downs in the early 1900s. Winn established betting machines set up at the track, giving it a source of income. He managed to convince some of the more prominent northern owners to enter their horses in the 1914 Derby, and he

Spectators crowd the track at Churchill Downs, awaiting the Kentucky Derby. The race shown here was run earlier on the same day as the 1983 Derby.
WIDE WORLD PHOTOS

was very accommodating to the press so that the race received plenty of good publicity. When a filly named Regret won the Derby in 1915, her rich and famous owner, Harry Payne Whitney, stated, "I do not care if she never wins another race or if she never starts another race. She has won the greatest race in America." His comment helped make the Kentucky Derby the best-known horse race in America. Today, any horse that wins this race has guaranteed its fame and fortune.

The Preakness is the second "jewel" in the Triple Crown. This race, run at Pimlico racetrack in Maryland, has followed the Kentucky Derby since 1932. It is run at a distance of 1 3/16 miles.

Jockey Donald Miller slows down his mount, Deputed Testamon, after winning the 1983 Preakness.
WIDE WORLD PHOTOS

Laffit Pincay, Jr. rides Caveat to a big win over Slew o' gold in the 1983 Belmont Stakes.
WIDE WORLD PHOTOS

The Belmont stakes, held at New York's Belmont Park racetrack, is the last of the three Triple Crown races. Public interest in this 1 1/2-mile race is especially high when one of the horses in it has already won both of the other Triple Crown races. Of the twenty-two horses that have won the Kentucky Derby and the Preakness, only half have captured the Belmont as well. Those eleven horses became classic champions and went on to make fortunes for their owners as sires.

Secretariat, believed by many to be the greatest racehorse of the century, won the Triple Crown in 1973, finishing far ahead of his competition in all three races. He was syndicated for $6 million, a record at the time.

PENNINGTON GALLERIES

When a stallion is especially valuable because of his racing record, his breeding career may be "syndicated." This means that his ownership is divided up into many shares. Each share represents one breeding to a mare. Since every year a stallion can be mated with thirty to fifty mares, the average number of shares in a syndication is forty. A famous stallion may be syndicated for over $20 million. In such a case, each shareholder pays half a million dollars for the opportunity to breed a mare each year to the stallion. If one of the shareholders in the syndicate has no mare, he receives money equal to the cost of a breeding instead.

The stallion is chosen with great care by the breeder of the mare, who needs to consider many factors. First, of course, is the stud fee. For economic reasons, breeders generally choose a stallion whose fee is about a fourth the value of the broodmare. The bloodlines of both the stallion and mare are very important. The breeder hopes to find a stallion whose traits will complement his mare's traits, so that the foal they produce together will combine the best of both parents.

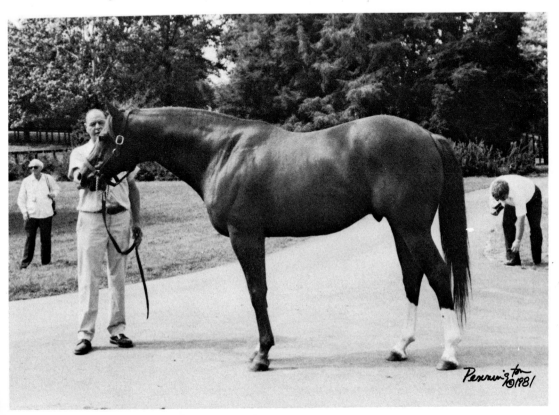

After a mare is bred to the stallion, she carries the growing foal in her body for eleven months. For the purposes of racing, all foals born in a year are given January 1 as their official birthday. Thus, a foal born in June would be officially a year old the following January, even though it would really be younger than seven months old. Because breeding Thoroughbreds costs so much money, owners want a return on their investment as soon as possible. That's why Thoroughbreds are raced as two- and three-year-olds, while they are still young and growing. Breeders want their foals born early in the year so that they will be as mature as possible when they begin racing. For this reason, many Thoroughbred foals are born in February and even January rather than in the springtime, when most baby animals come into the world. Sometimes breeders put mares that haven't been successfully bred that year in barns with the lights on for hours after dark. The horses' bodies are fooled into reacting as if it were spring rather than winter, and the mares come into breeding condition.

When a broodmare is ready to give birth, she is brought into a barn and put in a stall. She is checked often for signs that the birth is coming soon. Before the foal is born, the teats of the mare's bag, or udder, become waxy-looking and may begin to drip milk. This is a signal that the foal will appear within hours. At some Thoroughbred farms, a video camera is aimed at the mare so that she can be watched on a TV screen from the warm comfort of a house. When the foal is about to come, the mare usually lies down. Contractions of the uterus, which held the baby for eleven months, push it out, usually front feet first, into the world.

Thoroughbred broodmares await the birth of their foals in the springtime.
DOROTHY HINSHAW PATENT

A young foal nurses.
DOROTHY HINSHAW PATENT

The strength of a Thoroughbred's legs can already be seen in a young foal.
DOROTHY HINSHAW PATENT

After the foal is born, it stands up within a few minutes and soon is nursing hungrily from its mother's bag. Thoroughbred foals are big, weighing about 100 pounds. Their legs are so long that they are already about 60 percent of their adult height. For the first day, the new foal is kept in the stall with its mother, and both are closely watched. If all goes well and the weather is nice, they may be let out into a small, fenced field called a paddock for a few minutes on the second day. Since a Thoroughbred is such a costly animal, however, a veterinarian usually looks the foal over and pronounces it healthy enough to be insured before it is allowed out of the stall. As the foal gets older and stronger, it spends more and more time outdoors. But every evening the mares and foals are brought indoors into stalls to spend the night.

Mares and foals in a pasture on a sunny morning.
DOROTHY HINSHAW PATENT

Training the foal to trust people starts right away. Every morning, a tiny halter is slipped over the foal's head before it goes outside. The halter is removed later that day. Handlers guide the foal as it heads for the pasture when it is very young, so the foal experiences the gentle touch of human hands daily. In this way, the foal gets used to having contact with people right away and comes to trust them. A horse that does not trust people will be difficult to train later on and may never become successful at the track, even if it can run like the wind.

About nine days after her foal is born, the mare comes into heat, which means she is ready to mate again. If she is in good health and has healed completely from the birth, she may be bred at this time. Often, however, breeders wait another two or more weeks, until the mare is in heat again, before breeding her.

After the foal has shown itself to be healthy and strong, the mare and foal are turned out into a pasture with other mares and foals every morning. The foals grow fast and soon are running and playing together. They try nibbling at the grass, although most of their nourishment still comes from their mothers' milk. They also continue to receive plenty of attention and handling from people. Every month, their hooves are trimmed and they are given medicine to kill the worms that may live inside their digestive system. Every evening, they are brought into their stalls.

When the foals are about six months old, they are weaned—that is, taken off mother's milk. To accomplish this, the foals must be separated from their mothers. The female foals, called fillies, are kept in one pasture, and the male foals, or colts, are kept in another. The foals and mares are very upset about being separated, but they are kept far enough apart that they cannot hear one another's cries. The first night alone in the barn is frightening for the baby horse, but it soon gets used to life without its mother.

Once the foals are weaned, they are called weanlings until their "birthday" on January 1. Then they are called yearlings. These young horses have a carefree life in the pasture, exploring and playing, eating fresh green grass, and growing bigger and stronger every day.

Yearling fillies run free in their own pastures.
DOROTHY HINSHAW PATENT

Many small Thoroughbred farms, as well as some large and famous ones, like Calumet Farm, in Lexington, Kentucky, raise their own horses for racing. These stay-at-home animals are called homebreds. Two Triple Crown winners—Whirlaway and Citation—were Calumet horses, and so were many Kentucky Derby winners. But breeding farms, both large and small, often raise their horses to sell at auction as yearlings. Spendthrift, for example, is a 4,000-acre breeding farm in Kentucky that has forty syndicated stallions standing at stud. Among these are such famous racers as Triple Crown winners Seattle Slew (1977) and Affirmed (1978). The Spendthrift stallions are bred to about 2,000 mares each year. Many of these mares come from outside breeders, but dozens of them belong to Spendthrift and will produce high-quality yearlings that will be sold at auction.

Many auctions are held each year. Over 20 percent of Thoroughbred yearlings are sold at auction, and those sold are generally of high quality, with the potential of becoming successful racehorses. Buying a horse at an auction is a risky business. Just because a horse has fine breeding and a strong, promising body does not mean it will be successful at racing. Although a few horses earn plenty of money for their owners, most actually lose money. But people who buy at auctions are ever hopeful that they will take home a bargain like Seattle Slew, who sold for $17,500 and went on to win $1,208,726 and to be syndicated for $12 million! Another auction bargain was Spectacular Bid, bought for $37,000, who earned $2,781,607 and was syndicated for $22 million. On the other hand, it is easy to get stuck with a horse like Canadian Bound. This son of the great Triple Crown winner

Seattle Slew, a favorite with the crowds, was raced as a four-year-old instead of being retired directly to stud after his easy victories in the Triple Crown races in 1977. In the 1978 Marlboro Cup, he defeated the favorite, Affirmed, by three lengths. Here, Slew is being led into the winner's circle after beating his opponents by eight lengths in a race at New York's Aqueduct track.

WIDE WORLD PHOTOS

*Spectacular Bid, a powerfully built Thoroughbred, was
the all-time leading money winner when he retired as a
four-year-old, with $2,781,608 won in thirty races.*
WIDE WORLD PHOTOS

*The July Selected Yearling Sale is one of the most
important yearling auctions. This Northern Dancer sold for
$10.2 million in 1983, a record at the time.*
BILL STRAUS, KEENELAND ASSOCIATION

Secretariat was sold at auction for $1.5 million, yet he was a failure on the track. When he was three, Canadian Bound was retired to stud for a fee of only $1,000.

Some auctions are especially well known. Of the more than 7,000 yearlings auctioned yearly, between 500 and 600 are sold at the two most famous auctions—the July Selected Yearling Sale held in Lexington, Kentucky, in July, and the Saratoga Annual Yearling Sale, held in August in Saratoga Springs, New York. To be sold at one of these, a yearling must pass a very careful inspection for fine conformation—a body that promises success at the track— and must have an outstanding pedigree. The average sale price of yearlings at these events is over $150,000, and some go for well over $1 million.

Before the yearlings are auctioned, their owners hope that nothing bad happens to them. Horses' legs are easily damaged, and yearlings romp, gallop, and play with abandon. Thoroughbreds are raised to want to run, and to run even in the face of pain and danger. These traits, which help make

*This photo of a California yearling was taken
to show its conformation for auction.*
NORTHERN CALIFORNIA THOROUGHBRED ASSOCIATION

great racehorses, also can lead to accidents that result in a horse's injury or death.

The yearlings are carefully prepared for their big moment at the auction. They are taught to respond to being led and to stop and stand on command. They are groomed until their coats gleam in the sun. Grooming not only makes them beautiful, it helps teach them to trust humans. The yearlings' hooves are carefully trimmed and oiled, and they are fitted with lightweight horseshoes. They learn to walk into a horse van without fear, and they are driven around in the van so they become used to traveling from place to place. All this training will make the trip to the auction easier for the young horses.

*Racehorses must become used to being shoed, since their shoes
are changed every two to four weeks. Here Gary Bonde works
on a horse at Bay Meadows Raceway in California.*
BARBARA AND JOHN BAKER

The yearlings are brought to the auction site a day or two early so that possible buyers can get a good look at them. They are kept in stalls and are paraded out for people who come to examine them.

When it's time for the auction to begin, each horse is given a number. The actual sale takes only a few minutes. The horse is led before the possible buyers while the auctioneer describes its breeding and the racing accomplishments of its close relatives. Then the bidding begins. Sometimes the breeder sets a minimum price for the horse and the bidding starts there. The auctioneer keeps track of the bids with his singsong voice and does what he can to get the price as high as possible. When it is clear that the bidding will go no higher, the horse is pronounced sold. Now it has a new owner.

3

Training a Racehorse

Since they start racing as two-year-olds, Thoroughbreds must begin serious training while they are still young. At about a year and a half, when training usually starts, a typical yearling has reached 95 percent of its full height. However, its muscles are not completely developed and its bones have not reached their final strength and thickness.

Unfortunately, the term "breaking" is used for training horses for riding. "Breaking" sounds as if the animal is somehow damaged in the process. But when the training is done carefully, nothing could be further from the truth. A Thoroughbred is taught slowly, with patience and gentleness, so that its fine spirit and its confidence in itself and in people remain strong.

*The longe line is used to accustom horses to
a trainer's commands and for exercise.*
MARY COOLEEN, COURTESY OF WESTPORT NEWS

The first step in training is usually done on the longe (pronounced "lunge") line. The horse is taught to move in a circle, while the trainer stands at the center holding the line. The horse learns to follow the commands the trainer sends through the line. When the line is let out, the horse is to canter around the circle. When it is pulled in somewhat, the horse knows to trot. When the line is shortened more, the horse learns to walk.

As the horse gets used to the longe, it may be equipped with a bridle and saddle so it can become accustomed to a bit in its mouth and an object on its back. At first, a horse is likely to be afraid, but the trainer is always gentle and reassuring, patting it and talking softly so that the animal overcomes fear quickly.

Once the yearling is used to the saddle and bridle, it is "backed." This means it learns to have a rider on its back. Backing is, of course, a very important step in training a

*Thoroughbreds are galloped around the track
during training in Florida.*
FLORIDA DEPARTMENT OF COMMERCE, DIVISION OF TOURISM

horse. It is usually done in the Thoroughbred's stall, where the horse feels secure and where there are no distractions. The rider may first lie sideways over the saddle, just to give the yearling the feeling of weight. The trainer reassures the horse with touch and voice while it gets used to the feeling of weight on its back. When the rider can sit upright in the saddle without upsetting the horse, the animal is led around the stall so that it can adapt to moving while carrying weight.

Once it is comfortable with a rider, the horse is taken outside and ridden. It still has a lot to learn. It needs to know how to respond to the rider's hand signals, given through the reins to the bit in its mouth. It must feel completely at ease with a rider so that it can run with confidence. At first the young horses are often worked on the training track in the company of an older, gentle horse so that they see there is nothing to fear.

Getting a yearling to this point, so that it is used to being ridden and knows how to respond to its rider's commands, takes at least two weeks. Some horses learn more slowly than others and some are more fearful. Each yearling is treated as an individual and is trained at the rate it can handle.

Now the Thoroughbred yearling is ready to be conditioned for racing. It is slowly galloped around the track, for

increasing distances, to strengthen its muscles and to build up its wind. After a few weeks of this sort of training, called "being legged up," the horse may be breezed for the first time. When a horse is breezed, it is allowed to run fast. The trainer must be careful not to breeze a horse too soon, or it may hurt its young legs.

Another thing a Thoroughbred must be taught is familiarity with the starting gate. Races begin with all the horses shut into individual stalls in the gate. When the starting bell rings, the doors to the stalls fly open and the horses burst out running. At first, the starting gate is frightening to a young horse. It is a 16-foot-tall contraption of metal, with narrow stalls that confine the horses. Horses are naturally afraid of being trapped in a place they cannot get out of, so they must learn that the starting gate will not hurt them.

This photo of the start of the 1984 Kentucky Derby shows how quickly the horses must come out of the starting gate and how close they are to one another at the beginning of the race. Swale, who won the race, is number 10 over at the right of the photo.
WIDE WORLD PHOTOS

A racehorse in training is brought slowly up to the gate and allowed to sniff and examine it. Then the horse is led through one of the open stalls over and over again. After the Thoroughbred gets used to the gate, it learns to stand in a stall. Then it becomes accustomed to having the back door closed behind it and learns to take off, first at a trot and then at a canter. Eventually, it learns to stand with both doors closed and to dash out galloping when the bell rings and the front door springs open. Since races can be won or lost in the starting gate, this is a very critical stage in the development of a racehorse.

After the fall training session, the yearlings may be given a few weeks off to rest up before really serious work begins. On January 1, all the yearlings become two-year-olds and will be facing the beginning of their racing careers.

The two-year-olds are still very young, growing horses. Their bodies are like those of teenagers—almost full grown, but not completely formed and developed. Some of them are

These two-year-olds are taking a break from training. It is important not to work young horses too hard or they could develop serious problems with their legs.
DOROTHY HINSHAW PATENT

ready for serious training at the beginning of the new year, while others need to be brought along more slowly. Because their bones are still growing, young Thoroughbreds can easily hurt their legs, which can keep a horse from racing for weeks or even months.

The first races begin in the spring, so a horse that will be going to the track has a lot of work to do to get ready. A two-year-old that will be racing is breezed at increasing distances, starting with as little as one-sixteenth of a mile and working up to a half mile or so. It learns to run on the track with other horses. Trainers try to match young animals for ability when they run together so that a youngster does not get badly beaten. The two-year-olds need to know that they can win, or they may become discouraged and lose their confidence. Confidence and the will to win are just as important as speed on the track, for a racer must often push itself to the maximum to come out ahead in a race, where a fraction of a second can make the difference between winning and losing.

After proper training, a racehorse should have a lean, muscular body and an eager attitude. Trainers cannot make a horse perform better than its body and spirit will allow, but they can make mistakes that prevent a horse from living up to its potential. The horse must know how to break quickly from the starting gate and must be willing to follow the signals of its jockey, even though it is very excited by the race. It has to run straight on the track and must be able to run along the inside fence without getting too close or bumping into it. It needs to run its fastest, even when surrounded closely by other galloping horses.

A fine racehorse has many physical factors in its favor. Its hind legs are muscular and long. They provide the driving force for the running stride by reaching forward under the body and pushing off from the ground. The back must be strong, for it supports the rider and carries the force generated by the hind legs through the body. Its shoulders slope from the withers to the chest, giving the forelegs a long reach as they swing forward. The forelegs themselves must be sturdy and straight, since they carry the weight of the head and neck as the animal runs. If the front legs are at all crooked, so that extra strain is put on the knees, the animal is likely to injure its front legs while racing.

One stride of a racing Thoroughbred's gallop covers from 21 to 24 feet, about two and a half times the length of the body. All four feet are off the ground for part of a galloping stride. During this airborne period, the hind legs stretch forward. Then one strikes the ground and powers the body

This photo shows the strain placed on a horse's forelegs when it runs. The legs must be strong and straight in order to take the strain. CALIFORNIA THOROUGHBRED BREEDER'S ASSOCIATION

forward, followed by the other. As the second hind foot finishes its forward push, the opposite front foot hits the ground, followed by the other front foot. Then all four feet are in the air again as the horse gathers its body for the next powerful stride.

When a hoof lands, the tendons in the foot store energy like a spring, releasing it as the hoof leaves the ground. This helps give the animal its push as it gallops. A good racetrack will compress as the horses' hooves hit the dirt and will spring back as each hoof is raised. Such a springy track, which puts less strain on the horses' legs, allows them to run faster and more safely than one that is too hard or too soft.

Alternative track materials are being developed to make tracks safer for racehorses, and easier to maintain. In this photo, trainers Skip and Sally Brittle gallop their horses on a track composed of Fibar, a surfacing material made from wood fibers.
PHOTO BY CAPPY JACKSON, COURTESY OF FIBAR INC.

Affirmed, on the right, defeated Alydar, on the left, in all three of the 1978 Triple Crown races. Their exciting Belmont contest is shown here. The two gallant horses battled for the win all the way from the ⅜ milepost to the finish line, where Affirmed barely won. Many feel it was the greatest horse race ever. Steve Cauthen rode Affirmed to victory, while Jorge Velasquez piloted Alydar. THE NEW YORK RACING ASSOCIATION, INC.

A Thoroughbred runs at about 40 miles per hour. Because of the intense competition of racing, the spirit of the horse is just as important as its speed. Some horses want to get out in front of the others and run their fastest the entire race. These horses, called sprinters, can win short races but often tire before reaching a mile in longer races. Other Thoroughbreds, called stayers, are content to run more slowly until near the end of the race, when they put on a burst of speed and overtake the tiring sprinters. Staying power is much less common in Thoroughbreds than pure sprinting speed. It is also more valuable, for the most important races are run at distances of at least a mile.

A few great racehorses are sprinters, however. Affirmed, the 1978 Triple Crown winner, is such a horse. His racing style was to charge out in front at the beginning of a race and not to let another horse pass him. Few horses have the combination of strength, stamina, and heart that made a sprinter like Affirmed a consistent winner. Affirmed became the first Thoroughbred to win over $2 million. When he retired as a three-year-old in 1978, Affirmed was syndicated for $14 million.

4

At the Track

The final test of a racehorse, of course, is the race itself. In two minutes or less, the result of all the months of training for every horse entered in the race will be decided. By far the most money in a race goes to the winner, with decreasing amounts going to second, third, and fourth places. A few tracks also award a small purse to fifth or sixth place.

The amount of money won at a race, called the purse, varies tremendously. For example, in 1980, the Jockey Club Gold Cup at Belmont Park paid $329,400 to the winner, with a total purse of $549,000, while the Arlington Million, begun at Arlington Park in 1981, offers a total purse of $1 million, with $600,000 going to the winner. The 1980 Kentucky Derby paid $250,500 to the winner, while the Santa Anita

Handicap, run at Santa Anita racetrack in Arcadia, California, paid $190,000. Such races attract the best horses. A race for inferior horses, on the other hand, may have a total purse of under $2,000. Each racetrack has its own system for distributing the total purse. Belmont in 1980, for example, averaged 60 percent to the winner; 22 percent to second place; 12 percent to third; and 6 percent to fourth. Across the country, the winner receives somewhere between 55 and 65 percent of the total purse. A champion racehorse can win a great deal of money in one year. In 1979, Spectacular Bid pulled in $1,279,334, by coming in first in ten of the twelve races he ran that year. His wins included the Kentucky Derby and the Preakness.

Kinds of Races

The variety of races can be confusing. Entries to races are usually limited to animals that meet certain conditions. In general, male horses, especially young ones, can run faster than female ones. For this reason, many races are open to both sexes, while a few are restricted just to fillies and mares. There is even a Triple Crown for fillies, which consists of the Acorn, Mother Goose, and American Oaks. Fillies can enter the traditional Triple Crown races, too. In addition to the Kentucky Derby win by Regret in 1915, a filly named Genuine Risk took it in 1980. Entries may also be based on the horse's age, or on how much money it has earned. Some are restricted to animals bred in the state where the race is held.

Races involve two basic kinds of contests. By far the most numerous events are "claiming races." These pit the less glamorous majority of Thoroughbreds against one another.

John Henry, the biggest money-winning racehorse of all time, has collected over $5 million during his career.
CALIFORNIA THOROUGHBRED BREEDER'S ASSOCIATION

Fillies can sometimes win out over colts. Here, Genuine Risk is shown winning the 1980 Kentucky Derby, comfortably ahead of her opponents. WIDE WORLD PHOTOS

The animals that are running can be purchased or "claimed" by any qualified buyer before the race begins. There is a reason for this. Since the fans want each race to be exciting, with the outcome in doubt, there needs to be a way of making sure that the horses are roughly equal in ability. There are so many horses and so many races, it is impossible to check up on every horse. Therefore, the owners are kept honest by setting a price on their horses, and entering them in races with other animals considered to be the same value. The claiming race provides an incentive for the owner to put a fair price on his horse, because otherwise he might have to give it up. If, for example, his horse was worth $5,000, but he entered it in a $3,000 race, it would almost certainly win. However, the owner would probably lose his horse, since a buyer would spot it as a bargain—getting a $5,000 horse for $3,000. The claiming race system therefore keeps owners from entering horses in races where they would win against inferior opponents. The price set on claiming races ranges from under $2,000 all the way up to over $20,000. The majority of races in the United States are claiming races with a claiming price under $10,000. The higher the claiming price, the bigger the purse for the winners.

Stakes races, such as the seven races in the recently established Breeder's Cup competition, are designed to attract the finest horses with particular qualifications to the track. The best stakes are open to all horses of a certain age and possibly sex. Owners must pay to enter their horses in stakes. Generally, the horse must be "nominated" a few weeks or even months in advance. A fee ranging from $25 to about $250 is paid at that time. Any owner with a promising horse will nominate it for the biggest races. For example, 319 horses were nominated for the 1978 Kentucky Derby. By race day, however, most of the nominated horses are not entered, for the amount of extra money needed to actually race can be very high. The Kentucky Derby costs $7,500 in final fees to enter. The fees, plus an amount added by the track, form the purse for the race, which is divided up among the winners.

Before the Race

There is a lot more to the race than its actual running. About twenty minutes before the race, the grooms lead their horses to the paddock, the area where they will be saddled and mounted. The trainers and their assistants then saddle up the horses, while a veterinarian examines them to make sure they are fit to race. An official horse identifier also checks the number tattooed on the inside of the horse's upper lip to see that the right horses are being run. This is to keep dishonest people from substituting a different horse in order to make money from betting on the race.

Every racehorse must have its identification number tatooed inside its upper lip before it can be raced. Here, horse identifier Darrylle Sparks does her job. BARBARA AND JOHN BAKER

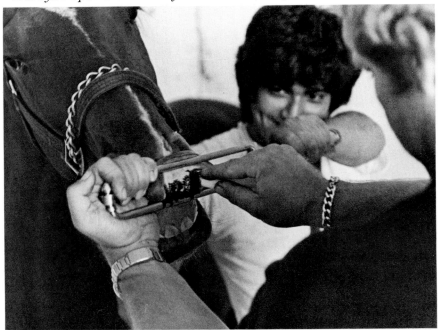

Ten minutes or so before the race, the jockeys mount the horses. Before that, each jockey has been weighed while carrying the horse's equipment. Every horse in the race carries an assigned weight, generally between 96 and 138 pounds. The more weight it carries, the harder it must work to win a race. In an "allowance race," the weight carried depends on a horse's age and record. For example, the basic weight for a three-year-old may be 116 pounds, while older horses may carry 122 pounds. Horses that have not won races recently may be allowed to carry less weight than the basic amount. In a handicap race, a track official called a handicapper determines how much weight each horse will carry in the race, based on its past performance. If the jockey and equipment do not weigh enough, lead weights are added to the saddle pad to bring the weight up. If the weight is too high, the public is informed over the loudspeaker, since it might affect the betting on the race.

In order to make the weight a racehorse carries so low, the saddle and jockey must be light. A racing saddle is hardly more than a place for the jockey to perch over the horse's withers. It weighs only three pounds and has small aluminum stirrups for the jockey's boots to fit into. Jockeys must weigh no more than 112 pounds, yet they need to be strong enough to control and stay positioned on top of a powerful, thundering racehorse. A jockey must also be brave, since race riding is a dangerous business. Few jockeys make it through their careers without broken bones or close calls.

Great jockeys need to be able to communicate with their mounts as well as to control them. They need to understand the racing styles of the horses they ride to take advantage of

The small racing saddle,
with its thin stirrups,
is very lightweight.
CALIFORNIA THOROUGHBRED
BREEDER'S ASSOCIATION

A few women,
such as Robyn Smith,
are successful jockeys.
NEW YORK RACING ASSOCIATION

49

Willie Shoemaker, shown here in 1967 in the winner's circle on the great horse Damascus, is famous for the way he communicates with horses through his delicate hands. His 6,072 wins set a record, and the money won by his mounts totaled $43,799,496.
NEW YORK RACING ASSOCIATION

their strong points and minimize their weak ones. A jockey's hands, as they hold the reins and feel the way the horse reacts to the bit in its mouth, hold the key to his ability to sense the mood of his mount.

After all the jockeys are mounted, the post parade begins. A bugle announces the entry of the horses with the famous cavalry call, and the racers enter the track. There they are met by lead "ponies" (actually full-sized horses) and their riders, who escort the racers in front of the stands during the parade. As the horses walk by, the announcer reads out information about them—name, owner, jockey, and so on.

After that, the horses are warmed up for the race. This exercise is very important, for their muscles must be warm and loosened for the tremendous strain they will undergo.

The horses are then led into the starting gate. This process can be tricky, for some animals are afraid of the gate, despite their training. A few must be backed in, and a rare horse must be blindfolded or it won't enter. Each horse has been assigned a "post position"—a starting-gate stall number—by a random drawing before the race. The number 1 position is on the inside rail, number 2 is next to it, and so forth. Each stall has its own door, but all the doors open at the same time when the starting bell rings. The gate mechanism is simple but effective. The halves of each door have springs that make the doors stay open. But the two halves also have opposite magnetic charges. As long as the electricity is on, the two halves remain stuck together. But when the current is turned off, the magnetic field is gone, and all the gates spring open at the same time.

Before the race, a lead pony escorts a racehorse around the track.
STEPHEN E. DEVOL/GOLDEN GATE FIELDS

The Race

Once all the horses are in the gate, the starter rings the bell and cuts off the electricity. The doors fly open and the horses leap forward. The race is on!

The best place for a horse to run is near the inside rail, since the curves are shorter and the distance around the track is therefore less. But not every horse can be on the rail, and as the horses surge forward, each jockey tries to get his mount into the best possible position. Some Thoroughbreds want to be in front, and others run best when they are away from the pack. A good jockey knows his mount's personality and does his best to work with the horse for a win.

Galloping full tilt along the track takes great strength and fitness. The horse breathes once per stride, and its heartbeat shoots from the resting rate of about 24 beats per minute up to 250. The forelegs are under enormous strain during a race. Each foreleg has seven different joints in which the bones press against one another during a stride. Each leg in turn must support the full weight of the horse, jockey, and equipment while the animal charges along at 40 miles per hour.

The easily injured front legs of a racehorse are protected by standing wraps when the animal is in its stall.
BARBARA AND JOHN BAKER

Because they are raced so young, American Thoroughbreds often suffer from serious leg problems. Their bones are not fully developed until they are four or five years old, yet they are expected to undergo the strain of racing when only two. Leg injuries are one of the most common causes of early retirement for a racehorse. But even with leg problems while young, a Thoroughbred can make big money for its owner. In 1984, for example, Devil's Bag, who had raced brilliantly as a two-year-old, was retired before the Kentucky Derby because he had a bone chip in his right knee. Despite his short racing career, Devil's Bag was syndicated for $36 million!

During a race, the jockey's goal is to keep the horse well positioned while letting it save enough energy for the all-important "stretch run" along the straight stretch just before the finish.

Near the end of a race, a sprinter that was out in front all the way from the start is likely to fade and finish far back in the pack. This is especially true in a race of a mile or more. A stayer that was running comfortably in the middle may turn

Angel Cordero, Jr., the famous jockey shown here, has won more than 5,000 races. NEW YORK RACING ASSOCIATION

The finish of a horse race is often very close. Without the special finish-line camera, it would be difficult to determine the winner.
PIMLICO RACE COURSE

In other races, the winner completely outdistances the opposition, as did the great horse Citation in the 1948 Preakness. This Triple Crown winner is considered to be one of the three greatest American racehorses, along with Man O' War and Secretariat.
KEENELAND-MORGAN

on its speed and rush forward to win. When two or more horses have energy for a final sprint, the race can get really exciting as they strain toward the race's end.

A special camera automatically takes pictures of each horse as its nose reaches the finish line. That way, there is an accurate record of the exact order in which the horses crossed. When the race is close, the film is used to determine the places of the racers. This is called a "photo finish." Every now and then, two or even three horses hit the finish line at exactly the same time, in a "dead heat."

After the winners have been determined, the first-place horse is led to the winner's circle, where the owners, trainer, and jockey proudly have their picture taken with their animal. Then the jockey dismounts and heads for the weight room to be checked again to make sure he carried the correct weight. The horse is taken to the test barn, where urine and blood samples are analyzed for illegal substances. Because so

The champion jockey, Eddie Arcaro, in the winner's circle on top of Nashua, who won the Preakness and Belmont in 1955. Arcaro rode for thirty-one years, and his mounts earned over $30 million. NEW YORK RACING ASSOCIATION

much money is involved in horse racing, both in the winner's purses and in betting, the race officials must do everything they can to see that the race was run honestly and fairly. Years ago, when track authorities were less thorough, horses were often drugged. For example, heroin was rubbed on a horse's tongue before a race. (This practice led to the use of the word "horse" as a slang term for heroin.) The second-place winner and some of the other horses are also checked for illegal substances. The stewards, who supervise the races, can demand that any horse submit to drug tests. Perhaps if a favored horse has run very poorly, the stewards may suspect that it has been given illegal substances to slow it down and may request that it be checked.

Horse racing was once a very corrupt business. Horses were drugged, jockeys were bribed, and other illegal activities were carried out to "make a buck." Just before the turn of the century, the Jockey Club was organized in an attempt to control racing. The licensing of all aspects of racing was taken over by this organization of fifty prominent people. But the public sentiment against corrupt gambling was not stopped, and in the early 1900s, state after state barred gambling on horse races. Racetracks lost money, and fans lost interest in the sport. Racetracks by the dozens closed down, and large numbers of horses and jockeys left the United States for Europe.

Racing in America was revived by the pari-mutuel betting system, in which legal betting takes place right at the track and can be controlled. Starting in 1908 and continuing through the 1930s, more and more states legalized these machines, and interest in racing skyrocketed.

Today, each state has a state racing commission that watches carefully over horse racing to minimize problems. The commissions now take care of licensing the sport, and the states cooperate with one another in their rules and decisions. Nowadays, the Jockey Club consists of ninety prominent Thoroughbred owners and breeders and has the responsibility of registering the horses, stables, and other participants in the sport, and decides on the rules of racing. Between the racing commissions and the Jockey Club, the sport of horse racing in the United States today is well controlled.

Life Between Races

Racehorses need time between contests to rest up, but they also need to stay in good condition to do well the next time they compete. The horses usually get a day off after a race, but then they must return to a conditioning program. The interval between races varies, depending on many factors. An inexpensive horse must run every two or three weeks to earn its keep. More valuable horses run in fewer races but can win much more money each time. If a horse is hurt it will need longer to recover than it otherwise would. With racing, as with early training, the trainer and owners must gamble on the soundness of their animals. A horse needs to race to make money, but its health is also important.

The grooms, exercise riders, and trainers are responsible for taking care of the horses and keeping them in the best possible racing trim. Life at the track begins at dawn, since early morning is the time for the horses' workouts. The animals are saddled and bridled and taken to the track. The type of workout depends on the condition of the horse and when it

Sometimes horses are exercised by "ponying"—the animal is led through its paces by a rider on another horse. That way, it doesn't have to carry any weight on its back but it still gets its workout. This is trainer Larry Richman at work at Bay Meadows Race Track in California. BARBARA AND JOHN BAKER

will next race. Sometimes a horse is simply "ponied" around the track—it is led by a rider on another horse and has no rider of its own. Horses may be worked in pairs or alone. At times, the trainer needs a timed run as this is necessary to prove the soundness of the horse to the racing officials. He must inform a track official, who then tells the official timers the name of the horse and the distance to be timed. Afterward, the time is published so that bettors can get an idea of

After it has cooled off, the horse gets a bath.
BARBARA AND JOHN BAKER

After their morning baths, the horses are hooked to the hot walker to dry off. As the horses go around in circles, the wheel to which their leads are attached moves with them. BARBARA AND JOHN BAKER

the speed of the horses in upcoming races. However, the trainer must be careful not to tire a horse during the time trial.

While the animals are working out, their stalls are thoroughly cleaned, and new straw is laid down for their health and comfort. Their bandages are washed every day, too, and they are given fresh hay and grain to eat. After the workout, the horse gets a bath. Then it is hitched up to the hot walker to dry off. The hot walker has a central post supporting a rotating wheel with long arms. A horse can be hooked on to the end of each arm. As the horses walk around, the wheel turns. That way, the horses can walk themselves. The hot walker may also be used to cool horses down after exercise.

When the horse is all clean and dry, it is led back to its stall, where it will spend the rest of the day. Fresh standing bandages are wrapped around its front legs. The saddle, blanket, and bridle used during the workout are cleaned daily after they are used.

Horses are social animals and enjoy the company of other living things. Many racehorses have a special friend, like this pygmy goat, that keeps them company during their long hours in the stall.
BARBARA AND JOHN BAKER

Racing in Europe

Thoroughbred racing and breeding are popular in many countries besides the United States, especially France, Ireland, England, Argentina, Canada, and Australia. In Europe, fewer races are held for two-year-olds, so not as many young animals are ruined by damage to their immature legs. British races and many races on the European Continent are held on grass surfaces rather than on dirt as in the United States. Grass is easier on a horse's legs than dirt, and recently, some American tracks have added turf (grass) races to their schedules. English races are run clockwise, while American races go in the counterclockwise direction.

Steeplechasing is a popular form of Thoroughbred racing in England and on some tracks in the eastern United States. Steeplechasing combines jumping skill with speedy running, creating exciting but dangerous racing. Horses and sometimes jockeys are seriously injured or even killed. The most famous steeplechase is the Grand National, run at Aintree, England, each year. It is the longest race, at four miles, and involves thirty jumps. The jumps take on different forms—ditches, fences, and fences with ditches. Some are especially tricky, such as Becher's Brook, a fence with a ditch that has a drop on the landing side. Horses tend to lose their balance and fall forward on landing.

Steeplechasing is a very challenging kind of racing.
Charlotte Brew, shown here in the 1977 Grand National, was the
first woman to ride in that great race.
WIDE WORLD PHOTOS

5

Thoroughbred Versatility

The vast majority of Thoroughbreds never succeed at the track—only about 2.5 percent become winners. Fortunately, Thoroughbreds also excel at activities besides racing, so an unpromising racer can find a place elsewhere. Thoroughbreds' sensitivity and spirit enable them to do well in several kinds of competitions, such as jumping and polo games. Many Thoroughbreds find work on the track, as lead ponies that guide the racers from the paddock or as mounts for the outriders that watch for trouble at race time.

Hunting

In Great Britain and in some parts of the United States, fox hunting is a popular activity for people who can afford it.

Most Thoroughbred horses
do not become racehorses.
Many, like this one, become
the prized companions of
children who may enter
competitions with them.
MARY COOLEEN, COURTESY OF
WESTPORT NEWS

*Mrs. John Glass and Mr. Pitner get ready
to hunt with Norfolk hounds.*
COURTESY OF MRS. JOHN GLASS

Riders gather, along with a pack of dogs called foxhounds, to follow the chase as the dogs pursue the scent of a fox through the woods. Usually a real fox is chased, but sometimes a person lays an artificial scent trail for the dogs to track. In Britain, crossbred horses are generally favored for hunting, but in the United States, pure Thoroughbreds are very popular. Crosses are sometimes made between Thoroughbreds and draft horses to produce strong and powerful hunters.

Hunt Jumping

Hunt jumping is an exciting horse-show event. The contestants all must complete the same course, which involves successfully jumping a variety of obstacles—one resembling a rail fence and another painted to look like a brick wall, for instance. The jumps are not particularly tall or difficult, and the horses are judged for their style. It is important that the horse keep its head low over the jumps and perform smoothly and naturally. With their elegance and beauty, Thoroughbreds are by far the most popular horse for hunt jumping in the United States.

Show Jumping

In show jumping, the horses are judged differently than in hunt jumping. Here, during the first round, the horses are eliminated if they knock down rails on three jumps. After the first round, the finishers are also judged on time, and the jumps may be raised to help determine a winner. The style of the horse in clearing the jumps is not important. But since time is taken into account, Thoroughbreds, with their inborn speed, are favored mounts.

Terry Rudd rides Rise and Rule over an obstacle
during the hunt jumping competition at the National
Horse Show in Madison Square Garden. NATIONAL HORSE SHOW

Charlie Weaver on top of Weather Permitting in the National
Horse Show. NATIONAL HORSE SHOW

Dressage

Dressage is a form of riding that dates back to the ancient Greeks. Over the centuries, dressage customs changed, and the event was refined into its modern form during the late eighteenth and early nineteenth centuries. The basic idea behind dressage is to develop a well-trained, obedient horse. Its gaits must be smooth and graceful, and it must respond perfectly to the commands the rider gives through his or her legs as well as through the bit.

The best-known dressage horses in the world are the Lipizzaners of the Spanish Riding School in Vienna, Austria. Show competition occurs throughout Europe and in North America. In these contests, horses and riders are judged on criteria such as how well the rider communicates instructions to the horse and how well it executes the movements. In novice or beginning dressage, the mount should perform basic movements with effortless, obedient grace. In Grand Prix competition, the top level of dressage, special challenging movements are performed. For example, in the pirouette, the horse must pivot on its hind feet as it turns in a circle. German and Swedish breeds, such as the Trakehner, are popular horses for show competition. In the United States, Thoroughbreds and Thoroughbred crossbreeds are used extensively in dressage.

With their graceful beauty, Thoroughbreds are naturals for the challenge of dressage. Here, J. Ashton Moore rides King's Praise.
BILL LANDSMAN ASSOCIATES, INC.

Polo

In the mounted ball game called polo, two teams of four players each try to score goals with a small, hard ball struck with a wooden stick. Polo originated in Asia and was brought from India to England in the nineteenth century. Today, the game is played in many countries, including the United States. It is a rich man's sport. Because of the physical demands placed on the animals, each player must have three horses.

The mounts are officially called polo ponies, although they are full-sized horses. In Britain, Thoroughbred crossbreeds are popular for polo, while in the United States, many pure-bred Thoroughbreds are polo ponies. These horses must be able to pound down the field at breakneck speed, stop, turn swiftly around, and dash back in the other direction. They must have some understanding of the game themselves, for the action is so fast that the rider often has no time to direct his or her mount.

Polo requires spirit and a competitive personality, both traits of the typical Thoroughbred. LONG ISLAND STATE PARK & RECREATION COMMISSION

6

Thoroughbreds and Other Breeds

Ever since its origin, the Thoroughbred has been used to improve and found other breeds of horse. Popular breeds in many countries, including the German Trakehner, Dutch Warmblood, and French Saddle Horse, were strongly influenced by the Thoroughbred. In North America, too, the Thoroughbred has made great contributions to the founding of several breeds developed to meet the needs of a young country.

The Morgan

The Morgan is perhaps unique among the American horse breeds. It began with one unusual stallion that lived in the late eighteenth century, now popularly called Justin Morgan.

(Justin Morgan was actually the name of a man who once owned the stallion.) Justin Morgan was small but very strong. He could outpull and outrun just about any other horse around, and he was beautiful as well. When this remarkable horse was bred to mares, he passed on his fine traits to the offspring, and a new breed was born.

We know little about the parentage of Justin Morgan, but some people believe his sire was a Thoroughbred stolen from the British during the Revolutionary War. Others believe that he was of Welsh Cob ancestry. Certainly, his stocky, strong body resembled a Welsh Cob's much more than a Thoroughbred's. But even if Justin Morgan's sire was not a Thoroughbred, Thoroughbreds have contributed to the development of the Morgan through the mares bred to Justin Morgan and through the horses bred to his descendants.

A Morgan stallion. WILLIAM MUÑOZ

An American Saddlebred. WILLIAM MUÑOZ

The American Saddlebred

The development of the American Saddlebred is woven into the early history of the United States. On the frontier, riding horses that could cover long distances without tiring, while providing a comfortable trip for the rider, were in great demand. Crosses among many breeds—Thoroughbred, Morgan, and breeds with different gaits, such as the Narragansett Pacer—were interbred to produce an attractive riding horse with great stamina. Early Saddlebreds were used extensively by the Confederate soldiers in the Civil War, and after the war they became popular show horses as well. In the late 1800s a breed association was formed, and a Thoroughbred stallion, Denmark, was named as the official foundation sire of the Saddlebred.

The Saddlebred performs special gaits during competition.
This is champion Kalanchoe, ridden by William Heuslein.
AMERICAN SADDLEBRED HORSE ASSOCIATION

The Saddlebred can move with two special gaits, the rack and the slow gait, in addition to walking, trotting, cantering, and galloping. The rack and slow gait are comfortable for the rider, since the horse moves up and down very slightly.

The Tennessee Walker

The Tennessee Walker, too, came about to cover long frontier distances with comfort for the rider. It developed later than the Saddlebred, from that breed and several others—Thoroughbred, Standardbred, and Morgan, for example. Unlike most other horses, the Walker reaches far forward with its hind feet when it walks so that the hind feet hit the ground in front of the hoofprints left by the front feet. This results in the unique Walker gaits—a long, striding walk performed either slowly or rapidly, leaving other horses behind in the dust, and an especially comfortable "rocking chair" canter.

The Standardbred has gone on from its Thoroughbred origins to become the greatest trotting and pacing breed in the world.
U.S. TROTTING ASSOCIATION

74

The American Standardbred

The American Standardbred is the finest trotting and pacing horse in the world. This breed originated with an English Thoroughbred stallion named Messenger, who was imported into the United States in 1788. Messenger carried the blood of all three Thoroughbred foundation sires and had run successfully in Great Britain. No one knows why, but Messenger's offspring produced unbeatable trotting horses. In those early days, trotting competitions were raced under saddle, whereas today in the United States they are carried out with the horses pulling a lightweight, two-wheeled cart called a sulky. The driver sits in the sulky and controls the horse through long lines to its bridle.

The greatest Standardbred sire was an especially powerful, unraced stallion named Hambletonian. He carried the blood of Messenger, but also of unknown horses and of the Norfolk Trotter breed. The first great trotter sired by Hambletonian was named Dexter. Dexter's mother was at least half Thoroughbred, and many of the other early Standardbreds were developed from Thoroughbred crosses. Today, both the sire and dam of a horse must be Standardbreds for it to be registered as a Standardbred. The Standardbred has in return been used around the world to improve the quality of harness horses, and it carries the blood of the Thoroughbred with it wherever it goes.

The American Quarter Horse

Perhaps the most famous American breed the world over is the Quarter Horse. It is actually the most popular breed in the world, with more than 1.5 million officially registered horses. Quarter Horses are used to work cattle in many countries besides the United States, especially Australia. While the origin of this breed lies in its ability to run a quarter mile faster than any other horse, its later development and improvement was as a cattle horse.

The first Quarter Horses, with their unrivaled sprinting ability, were bred by the early settlers. In those days, straight, even roads were rare. Flat, cleared areas were usually short in length, and it was over such short distances—down the main street of town, for example—that the settlers raced their horses for sport. The fastest sprinters won and were bred to produce more fine sprinters.

As with other American breeds, the Quarter Horse

The American Quarter Horse is the most popular breed in the world. This young stallion shows the strong Thoroughbred influence on racing Quarter Horses. WILLIAM MUÑOZ

derived from a mixed ancestry. But perhaps the most famous early Quarter Horse sire, Janus, was an imported Thoroughbred stallion of small size but powerful muscles that was brought to Virginia in 1756. Janus himself was an endurance horse that had won many four-mile races. When he was bred to Thorougbred mares, he produced horses like himself that ran fast over long distances. But when he was bred to native American horses of mixed ancestry, the result was fast sprinters with especially strong hindquarters.

Thoroughbred Contributions Today

While the Thorougbred figured prominently in the development of many breeds, it is still used to modify other breeds. A half-Quarter Horse foal can be registered as a Quarter Horse if the other parent is a Thoroughbred and if the horse has been successful at Quarter-Horse competition. Racing is once again popular for Quarter Horses, and a great deal of money can be won by these speedy sprinters. Many racing Quarter Horses are largely of Thoroughbred breeding, and racing Quarter Horses are coming to look less and less like powerful, muscular cattle horses and more like sleek Thoroughbreds.

Another American breed, the Appaloosa, also is changing, since breeding to either Quarter Horses or Thoroughbreds is allowed. Appaloosas are famed for their colorful spotted coats and are popular as pleasure and cattle horses. But they are also used for racing in some western states, and racing Appaloosas carry much Thoroughbred blood. American Paint Horses, too, which have blotches of white and dark colors, can have some Thorougbred ancestry if their coats are "paint" in color.

It is clear that the Thoroughbred horse, bred for speed and the will to win, is more than just a racehorse. It is a spirited, beautiful animal capable of passing on its good traits to its offspring whether it is bred to another of its kind or to a different sort of horse. It is hard to imagine what the world's horses would be like today if the Thoroughbred had never come about.

American Triple Crown Winners

Sir Barton	1919
Gallant Fox	1930
Omaha	1935
War Admiral	1937
Whirlaway	1941
Count Fleet	1943
Assault	1946
Citation	1948
Secretariat	1973
Seattle Slew	1977
Affirmed	1978

Suggested Reading

Nonfiction

Anderson, C.W. *Thoroughbreds.* New York: Macmillan
    Publishing Co., 1947.

Anderson, Clarence W. *Twenty Gallant Horses.* New
    York: Macmillan Publishing Co., 1965.

Biracree, Tom and Insinger, Wendy. *The Complete Book
    of Thoroughbred Horse Racing.* Garden City, New
    York: Doubleday, 1982.

Osborne, Walter D. *The Thoroughbred World.* New York:
    World Publishing Co., 1971.

Wilding, Suzanne and Del Baso, Anthony. *The Triple
    Crown Winners: The Story of America's Nine
    Superstar Racehorses.* New York: Parents Magazine
    Press, 1975.

Fiction

Farley, Walter. *Man O'War.* New York: Random House,
    1962.

Henry, Marguerite. *Black Gold.* Chicago: Rand McNally &
    Co., 1957.

Henry, Marguerite. *King of the Wind.* Chicago: Rand
    McNally & Co., 1948.

Magazines

The Blood-Horse
P.O. Box 4038
Lexington, Kentucky 40544

The Horseman's Journal
6000 Executive Boulevard
Suite 317
Rockville, Maryland 20852

The Thoroughbred Record
P.O. Box 4240
Lexington, Kentucky 40544

Glossary

allowance race: A race in which each horse is given a number of pounds to carry, depending upon its racing record. The better its record, the heavier the weight.

auction: A sale at which something is sold to the highest bidder. Many Thoroughbreds are sold at auction.

backing: In horse training, getting a horse used to the feeling of a rider on its back.

blinders: Leather cups that are attached to a bridle or head covering which allows the horse only to see in front of itself.

bloodlines: The hereditary background—the parents and other ancestors—of a racehorse.

breaking: Training a horse to accept the saddle, bridle, and rider so it can be ridden.

breeze: A fast run of a racehorse in training.

broodmare: A female horse used for breeding.

claiming race: A race in which the horses running can be purchased by a qualified buyer for a specific price.

colt: A young male horse.

conformation: The physical appearance of an animal.

dam: The mother of an animal, such as a horse.

dressage: The training of a horse to obey commands given to it by the rider through the reins and legs and, in advance dressage, by a trainer who is not riding the horse.

filly: A young female horse.

foal: A baby horse.

foundation sire: A stallion to which all members of a particular horse breed must trace their bloodlines.

groom: A person responsible for taking care of a horse.

half-breed: A horse that has one parent belonging to a particular breed.

halter: A headpiece for a horse to which a lead rope can be attached.

hand: A measure of a horse's height, a hand is four inches. The height is taken by measuring the number of hands from the ground to the top of the withers.

handicap: The amount of weight carried by a horse in an allowance race.

homebred: A horse bred by the same stable that races it.

jockey: The rider in a horse race.

lead pony: A horse that is used to lead a racehorse onto the track and parade it by the stands.

legging up: The training that strengthens the horse's muscles and increases its wind in preparation for racing.

longe line: A long lead line used to train horses. The longe line is attached to the horse's halter, and the trainer stands in the center of a circle around which the horse moves in response to the trainer's commands.

pari-mutuel betting: Racetrack betting in which the amount bet, minus costs, is divided among the winning bettors.

pedigree: The listing of the parents, grandparents, and so on, of an animal; its bloodlines.

photo finish: The finish of a race when it is so close that a photograph is used to determine the winner.

post parade: The parade in which horses are walked in front of the grandstand while the announcer gives their names, owners, and so on, before a race.

post position: The number of the starting gate stall assigned to a horse from a random drawing before a race. The horses wear numbers which correspond to their post positions.

purse: The total amount of money which is divided among the top placing horses in a race.

sire: The male parent of a horse.

sprinter: A horse that likes to get out in front at the beginning of a race.

stakes race: A race for which the horses' owners must put up money in order to qualify the animals for the race. Stakes races are generally for the better horses racing on a particular track.

stayer: A horse that prefers to wait until near the end of a race to put on speed.

steeplechase: A race during which the horses must jump over barriers.

steward: A racetrack official who, among other things, is responsible for determining the official winners of a race.

stud: A male horse that is used for breeding.

syndication: The dividing up of the breeding rights to a stallion into shares, usually numbering around forty. Normally, only very valuable stallions are syndicated.

tail-male line: The tracing of only the line of male ancestors of a horse—its sire, the sire's sire, and so on.

Triple Crown: The Kentucky Derby, Preakness, and Belmont stakes, all American races for three-year-olds. A horse that wins all three races gains a special place in racing history.

wean: To take an animal off its mother's milk.

winner's circle: The place to which the winning horse is led after a race, where its picture is taken along with the owners, trainer, and jockey.

withers: The top of the shoulder of a horse.

yearling: A one-year-old animal. A racehorse becomes a yearling on January 1 of the year following its birth, no matter what its real birthday is.

Index